S0-BUA-368

# THE ISLAND'S ONLY ESCAPE

*Poems by*

# MATTHEW PHILLIPS

)(

Pleasure Boat Studio: A Literary Press
Seattle, Washington

The Island's Only Escape
By Matthew Phillips
Copyright © 2017 by Louis Phillips
All Rights Reserved

ISBN 978-0-912887-57-9

Cover Design by Ian Phillips
Interior Design by Lauren Grosskopf

Pleasure Boat Studio books are available
through your favorite bookstore
and through the following:
SPD (Small Press Distribution) Tel. 800-869-7553
Baker & Taylor 800-775-1100
Ingram Tel 615-793-5000
Amazon.com and bn.com

and through
PLEASURE BOAT STUDIO: A LITERARY PRESS
www.pleasureboatstudio.com
Seattle, Washington

Contact: Lauren Grosskopf, publisher
pleasboatpublishing@gmail.com

# THE ISLAND'S ONLY ESCAPE

But learning, in the end, is like that:

a kind of island.

Plus the island's only escape.

*–"Sabbatical Island," Matthew Phillips, 1985-2011.*

All who joy would win must share it.

Happiness was born a Twin.

*– Lord Byron, 1788-1824.*

Ian and Matthew Phillips (1990)

"I sit with Shakespeare, and he winces not. Across the color line I move arm and arm with Balzac and Dumas, where smiling men and welcoming women glide in gilded halls. From out of the caves of evening that swing between strong-limbed Earth and the tracery of stars, I summon Aristotle and Aurelius and what soul I will, and they come all graciously with no scorn nor condescension. So, wed with truth, I dwell above the veil."

*W. E. B. Du Bois*
*The Souls of Black Folk*

# $\mathcal{F}$OREWORD

IF I STOP AND TRY TO REMEMBER PRECISELY WHEN I MET ANY of my students, I almost always draw a blank. The ones who make the strongest impressions on me don't usually do so right away. A few weeks into the semester a student will make an insightful comment or a memorable joke, and, for the first time, I'll notice him or her as something more than a name on an attendance list. But most of the time, even these moments don't stick in my mind, not even in the case of the students I get to know very well.

With Matt it was different. I can remember the day in October of 2003 when I was out in front of the Library Tower, getting a breath of fresh air, idly musing about something or other, and a husky-voiced, tall, poised and surprisingly polite student I didn't recognize introduced himself to me. He had a question about Napoleon, whose relationship to the Jews was covered in the assigned readings in my modern Jewish history class.

I don't remember exactly what Matt asked me, but I remember how surprised I was by the fact that Napoleon was far more than just a name to him, or a stick figure. He really knew something about his career and his relationship to the ideology of the French Revolution. Something about Napoleon's attitude to the Jews struck Matt as odd, and he wanted me to clarify it.

What was this kid doing in my introductory course? When he identified himself a freshman, I was stunned. I recovered a bit when he told me about the unusually good high school he had attended in Manhattan, but that only slightly reduced my surprise at encountering a new student who was so knowledgeable and articulate, and so mature.

From then on, I was always aware of Matt, watching to see his reaction to things I said in class, waiting to hear his questions. He was always thoughtful, always intensely engaged, ever more informed and mature, and always very formal and reserved. I liked that old-fashioned side of him and respected him for it. Even after he graduated, he still treated me a little deferentially. He wasn't someone I could easily induce to call me by my first name.

I looked forward to the day that that would happen. As Matt took his first, cautious steps into graduate work in Middle Eastern history, I was expecting a lot from him, and easily imagined the day when we would be colleagues and friends. I expected him to write important things. He had, indeed, already begun to do so.

Anyone who has ever written a letter to the New York Times knows how slight the chances are of ever seeing it in print, especially if you're responding to something in the weekend book review section. That's even more the case if you're complaining about a big shot. Matt was doing just that in May 2010, when he vented his disagreement with the celebrated Yale professor Harold Bloom's review of a new book on anti-Semitism. He wasn't alone. Unusually, the Times printed on May 21 ten responses to Bloom's review—with Matt's on top, probably because it was the most penetrating and the most eloquent. Matt wasn't afraid to accuse the venerable professor of "an appalling lack of discrimination." That may not sound very polite—but it was quite mild, I'm sure, compared to what Matt was thinking.

I have always had a tin ear and a thick skull for poetry, and can say nothing to illuminate the contents of this chapbook. But I'm glad that it exists, like the bench dedicated in his memory in Riverside Park, as a permanent marker for Matt. For those of his friends who are not, like me, mere Philistines, I'm sure that it will mean much more.

– Allan Arkush, Professor of Judaic Studies,
SUNY Binghamton

# Contents

## Letter From San Francisco

You were right—it is not China here.

I came to California and am getting California.

So what I'm not doing: learning Mandarin, eating dog.

But—I'll tell you—there are many hills,

And the other day, I passed a man struggling

Up one and was startled by how much he looked

Like me. There are no ancient wonders,

Only that golden bridge and a prison—

Imagine it! Suspended in the middle of water.

True, from a distance, it is almost comically small;

But to a prisoner there is blue in every direction

And to a child it must be halfway to China.

## In Mafia Films

Generations have a seamlessness here unreflected

In our lives. The baby screaming at his baptism

Will, we know, one day shoot a man as his

Brain spills all over what was, seconds ago,

The best he had outside of that trip to Italy.

The Priest, holding his tiny head, has known his

Father since he was a boy in Sunday School.

Now, as an adult,

He seems to draw his own conclusion

About the Good Samaritan. No matter,

The Church isn't all for substitute teachers.

Plus who cares about worldly questions?

Most men, Mafia films say, either get parking tickets or they don't.

They adjust their ties and take all kinds of mockery,

Fantasizing about strip-clubs where you always meet

And a back room where the fuckin' guy who slighted you pays.

## Another House

Maybe another house isn't a good idea.
After all, the low ceilings here have gotten
Us this far. The peeling paint, the paint's dull color,
Have made us—well, that's a bit of a stretch, but—
It has let us know where we are,
Which is not only some space we have passed through
But also, in the end, a kind of home.

There, on the other hand, the same things will be placed
In a new way, and I can't picture how that will look.
Though I know it's something desirable, is it possible
That we will get too much "natural light"?
Is there such a thing? Who really knows what will happen then?
We can't know until we are living there.
Unwrap the silverware from the newspaper, return the boxes
To the liquor store. Tell our friend with the van to sleep in.
Leaving won't soon be considered again.

## Chess

The young sergeant says, "War is like it";
Generals nod gravely, in agreement.

The single woman says, "Dating is like it,"
Referencing male intentions, and their concealment.

The college counselor says, "Applications are like it,"
Meaning plan ahead, if you want to be collegiate.

All these people know chess? It's hard to believe.
To the players it means the game itself.
When it's over, they tend to get up and leave.

## Driving Down

Mutual friends recommended the campsite.
It fulfilled what small promises were made so
They packed rented things into the car in order
To drive down. What they would do with the
Next long weekend was an unredeemed promise
And a lapse from ordinariness
That neither asked for. So much of it was in
The waiting that it wasn't worth considering;
So they drove away and back to themselves and
The much-joked-about "dwindling rations" gave way
To unpaid bills.

## Flight of the Peacemaker

As an American, he was told to take
The telescope rather than the magnifying glass;
It's History's long view that matters here.

As a final gesture, one tribal leader spat at
The other and tore up papers between them.

Everything was going. He tried to make
The place fit his sense of it. In the end,
It was like a man who fears poverty so much
That he leads the most impoverished life.

The next day, his plane took off.
The press was nowhere; when the propellers
Lashed out, their immediate wind made no
Impression. The landscape was made of wind.

He saw, as he rose, three giraffes in the foreground.
It became clear, looking at their bodies
Long above ground, what it was to live openly
And in a place without interiors.

## Fragments from Future Textbook

Their children listened almost perfectly; doctors made
Little use of talk-therapy and Ritalin.

They adapted their elderly to computers; libraries lent
Laptops to even arthritic senior citizens.

They mastered saving time, planning wars and the
Inevitable memorials simultaneously.

They loved their neighbors, mowed each other's lawns and
Built fences accordingly.

### Idea of the Wailing Wall

Without tone, or inflection, walls go up and stay.
Here is far from imagination's bend, a student's shape
Of handwriting, where a teacher can only shrug and say,
"It's anyone's guess." This is a known
Place of purpose. But ideas have purpose. Not unlike
Grave men in an image I have, rocking here.
There is a boy behind them with a shaped stone
Asking, "How far can it skip?" and "When do we
Go home?" A river behind him rocking with
No reference to the stone or what it makes for men,
The lasting quality of walls.

## Language

Unlike tractors, words stand ready to be used

Without that need for cornfields. They are like shells

Of ideas. The other day,

I said to a friend "always blue and endless, never rains".

She said, "sky".

I said, "you know, I have a terrible time describing what I think."

She said, "try."

## Letter From Sparta

The boy in the bunk next to me doesn't fit in.

He misses his mother. She sent him a package of

Soups, medicine, baklava, you name it.

Be here some time A.D.

I think he's more Persian material.


Basically, we plunder these cities and take their women.

They love me in my uniform.

Best of all, like the brochure said, I get to see the world.

Strange: in one village they read Aristotle;

Others gather to chant "Give Peace a Chance."

I asked my commander what this meant.

He said, "If you like to ask so many questions

You should fight for the Athenians."

## Neighbors

Seem to have a kind of genius for

Knowing the weather, taking out garbage,

Appearing in bathrobes.

Catalogues stack in front of the door and

We know they are gone. Twice you see into the apartment—

Returning mixed-up mail—but only note

The library's boldest titles.

Pictures in the hallway have other people,

Part of a life lived away from next-door.

This is, at last, what they have been leaving and

Coming to all these years. It has, you think,

A kind of sense to it now. Then the door shuts.

Along with keys, this is the neighbor's sound.

## New Year in the Desert

Each day, it's said, is basically the last.

Time is but a million sandstorms every minute,

What people, if they lived here, might call alarm clocks.

But once a year, the local conversation turns to resolutions:

The mountain, considering northern trends, wants to be seen

As "snow-capped." The cloud pledges to ditch its silver lining,

Calling it "a distraction from my distinct image."

**November 10<sup>th</sup>**

Came very close to falling asleep early.

Began to think about the next day, Thursday,

Nothing much happened so it faded into evening.

Leave the library, run into you,

Offer dinner, you accept, walk you home, say

Goodbye. I walk away, and twenty or thirty years ago,

So we've been told, all the organic food stores

Were used bookstores, though memory, when

It comes to an old neighborhood, tends to implant

More affordable, less snobbish things in its wake.

It's important to remind ourselves, I think, how it

Used to be, though we've never seen pictures, or spoken

To a native. It's a small country everyone has read about but no one

Has been to and there is, therefore, no danger of anyone contradicting us.

At this point, you come running up, startled, and say

"Tomorrow I'm leaving" or "I'm sick of how

You talk about my friends." In either case, we can

Either stand here and talk or

We can do so tomorrow, unless you are leaving; hardly matters.

We've learned change comes rather slowly,

As to old neighborhoods, and the fact that

You ran out of the door after I said goodbye to you is

Clearly foremost in your mind, I can tell. The statements

Might be incidental. I'm right next to the train station.

There is also one seven blocks

Away which I can walk to. At this point, I fell asleep.

## Sabbatical Island

Against his wishes, Dad took you to what he dubbed

"Sabbatical Island": communities of primitives are

His expertise, apparently.

Plus this one has the last vestige of a people.


His argument: that the island exemplifies

A perfect vantage point, a view

Unalloyed by perception, the distortion that

Comes from just looking. What the

Philosopher Thomas Nagle calls "the view

From nowhere."


And so on this island, it seems,

Where Dad, today, was yelling at a

Graduate student back home to

"Check something against the original."

How much could either of them really know?

But learning, in the end, is like that: a kind of island.

Plus the island's only escape.

## Said The Writer

He agreed to be interviewed after his last book.
We ran through his childhood; he looked down at
The coffee table and told me some story
About how he went to this river by his house. His father
Worked thankless hours so he went to this river
Alone and began to build. First it was a raft,
"Which was the first time," he said, "that I saw
Myself as a maker," He paused.

I myself was beginning to dislike him.
The whole thing held out a strange opportunity
That wouldn't be easily realized, if at all.
I tried to remember the themes of his work; certainly memory
And how it changes the past was a big one.
Plus the passage of time.

He was growing impatient so
I looked at my questions. In the last few weeks
They became clever, and knowing, became answers
In their own right. I shouldn't have made

Them to stand alone. Perhaps that would have

Prevented his room from taking on an unreal quality.

Certainly I've never, to use his word, been much of a "maker."

He smiled, went to get a drink and came back.

 "Look, what I'm trying to say is that in this art I can be

Someone else, namely wholly myself."

## Storm Season

One sign that what happened

Is important beyond the scene itself

Goes as the last cameraman climbs

Into the helicopter to return home. There is some

Chance that his cargo shorts will get caught in the

Propellers, creating, you think perversely, a local and

More immediate emergency. But the moment passes.

Life's uncertainty, a rule for understanding some punishment

Of people, does, at times, protect. The moment is unlike a

Storm, then: rising safely, leaving no debris, releasing itself

Only to arrive again for the next storm,

Of which the last can only be understood

As the final one for now, the closing of a season.

## The Caves of Lascaux

One teacher said to us, "Look, everyone, just draw what you know"—
So half the class did the bison and chasing,
The other half, a human and arrow.

Another teacher said to us, "See, art, it's the consummate human
endeavor"—
So the whole class understood that here at Lascaux
Man invented drawing, then He invented tenure.

## The Current Academic Climate

Seeing Logic and Systems of Governance for sale
On the street, he picks it up; the student who owned
It started off underlining, then stopped in chapter three.
The back flap shows his picture,
His stare is direct, his smile is halfway—
At that time, a mentor even spoke,
In earnest, of his "journey."

Flipping through the pages, he sees "this class sucks"
Written in the margins. Well, it's true, he says to himself, I
Have caught a lot sleeping recently.
But there have been so many cuts, plus the
Students seem younger—none of this is really related.
His mind has been going in a million different directions lately.

At the meeting, all the talk was of the current academic
Climate. It's pretty bad. But in twenty years,
Has it been good? Maybe most of my former students are dead,
He thinks. Then he begins to remember that
First year he was on the campus. There was an unbelievable number
Of girls everywhere; they huddled outside the library
In the fall; they seemed to be birds together

In their indecipherable sounds. Waiting for them to do something
Out of sync was like watching for metal falling from the sky.
He remembers all the time he spent outside of the library,
At peace, seeing in some an open sense of beginnings
And in others fleeting looks of recognition.

## The Great Man to the Historian

Know that when I sleep, they sleep, but nervously.
When I awake, the masses breathe a sigh of relief.
Culture and Commerce come to a virtual standstill
Til I get on my feet.


Once, I went to the theatre to see the town's rendition
Of Romeo and Juliet.
The papers asked "did you like it?" I responded.
They made some adjustments, and had Juliet shoot Romeo
In the head.

## The Latest Town

Shop owners hang their daily hours before
The shops are open.

Buildings, still window-less, advertise
Views to the town over.

The traffic circle's cement hardens.
No one marks in it their initials.

People bring cars is the guiding idea,
Parks are built.

A large cemetery remains.
Driving up, it looks like a war was fought long ago
And we were good enough to bury the other side's dead.

## To the Budding Anthropologist

You say, "They only work frantically, treating time like water in a drought."
Time is something you have more of. I hope it never peters out.

"They see history as something to be forgiven, or perhaps to be overcome."
The past is something to lord over others. I hope you profit from the ransom.

"They pass wisdom on through stories, one generation to the next."
You pass wisdom on the other way. Wonder how you approach sex.

Anyway, as tribal chieftain, let me tell you about our post-doc fellowship:
It consists of finding four-leaf clovers, and carrying mangoes.

And be careful in your translations, because when we use the word
"Fire" we mean not only the flame, but the light it shows.

## What is History

What is history? E.H. Carr asked.

Well, one possible answer is that history is

Two big ships headed for one another,        ·

People diving off the sides and the

Two captains—one not really paying

Attention; the other just happy to

Be in the middle of all those waves,

All that wind.

## Last Days

In the library, a girl curls up with Why People Get Sick.

Her boyfriend dozes happily.

Behind them, stacks stretch into

White halls of space; pages glisten from not being thumbed.


The other day, a boy eating with his mother

Overhears a man declare these the last days

Of winter, with a confidence he is used to from dad.

To mom, the sun means being bronze;

To him there is nothing cosmetic about it—

Sun is the big reason for snowless fields

Which are being plowed in his mind, ripening with all the

Promise of hitting and throwing; bases, after all these months

Are an unused white, like classroom chalk.


Behind him, the store-cat yawns on the windowsill

And the TV-weatherman puts a cold front where he will.

## Chat with a Professor

At the back of a less-than-crowded lecture,

A professor sits behind me. "A friend to Israel, he's ambulatory," he says,

"Brilliant scholar. Kind of a religious dove. Head of the

Philosophy Dept at Hebrew University.

A Neurologist has told his family not to expect much,"

"That's terrible," I reply. "It explains the long face."

"No, that's just the late hour," and he goes to play professor

Or to greet the Holocaust survivor speaking

Without betraying his tiredness. The man talks about Nazis,

the Gestapo, stealing false papers, something about

A "righteous Gentile" who has "no monument," selling

 stolen raincoats

To unwitting Germans. Stuff of survival.


What a weird thing it can be, just learning,

To have remoteness wiped away, only

By listening—comatose professors,

Jews in war, exiled families—as if these mandate our knowing.

Such extremes brought to us. Glimpses at suffering

Without wading in it. Closed books at our disposal;

"Survivors" who don't resent mostly captive audiences;

Memoirs that can be interrupted by doing something better

With the unfulfilled night—such conveniences,

But also how spoiling

To imagine "history" is always just far off

In Jerusalem, or that it is bald-headed, has a Polish accent

And is only presented after a warm introduction.

## Daylight Savings

He is not really happy—just today,

He spit twice on a window and watched it race down.

Friends are at that summer camp on the East Coast;

One letter tells him sports are just amazing there—

How high the nets—

Plus the girls, proportionally, are not like the ones at home

Who won't talk to him and are anyway flat-chested.


His father is sick of farming, almost looks forward to the harvest.

But he doesn't protest time, doesn't call town meetings

Or petition forces-at-large for shorter days.

On the playground, there is never talk of summers

Too long

No one looks forward to less corn.

## Coming to Larkin by Way of Auden

Coming to Larkin by way of Auden,

You drive a long road and turn right.

In your rear-view mirror is history,

Books with footnotes, religions,

Large moral decisions

And armies; they have gathered

And you should pick a side.

But then you drive in,

Open the door. Nothing is arresting anymore,

Just the ordinariness of having a life,

Of being yourself; you know you couldn't be happier

Without being someone else.

MATTHEW PHILLIPS WAS BORN AND RAISED IN New York City. He graduated from Bard High School Early College (BHSEC) in downtown Manhattan in 2003, earning an Associate's Degree in lieu of a High School Diploma at the age of 18. He earned a Bachelor's Degree at the State University of New York at Binghamton and from there enrolled in the CUNY Graduate Center where he was slated to earn a Master's Degree in Middle Eastern Studies.

As a reader and writer of poetry, Matthew found his subject matter through a variety of topics, from the joy of learning to the game of chess. However, his primary focus in writing was the Israel-Palestine conflict. Often critical of Israel's involvement in the war, he published eight such essays from 2010-2011 through Mondoweiss, an online platform dedicated to informing the public about the ongoing struggle for peace in the region.

He is the son of Louis Phillips and Patricia Ranard, and the twin brother of Ian Phillips. He died in New York City on April 4th, 2011, at the age of 26.

CPSIA information can be obtained
at www.ICGtesting.com
Printed in the USA
BVHW092249221220
595993BV00004B/59